Woven Basket
Egypt

Egyptian women wove baskets from the reeds that they found along the Nile River. The women used the completed baskets to carry supplies. They sometimes balanced them on their heads as they walked from place to place.

Literature Connections

The Egyptian Cinderella by Shirley Climo; Crowell, 1989.
Rimonah of the Flashing Sword by Eric Kimmel; Holiday House, 1995.
Temple Cat by Andrew Clements; Clarion Books, 1996.
Zekmet, the Stone Carver by Mary Stolz; Harcourt Brace Jovanovich, 1986.

Make a Woven Basket

Variations using two different mediums are provided to accommodate availability of materials. Variation 1, the more authentic version, uses basketry materials available in art supply stores or through art supply catalogs. In variation 2, poster board is substituted for flat reeds and yarn or string for round reeds.

▶ Materials

variation 1:
- reeds for weaving
  - 1/4" (.6 cm) flat reed - 24 feet (8 m)
  - 1" (2.5 cm) flat reed;
    - cut four 20" (51 cm) strips
    - and two 15" (38 cm) strips
  - #2 round reed - one 42"
  - (1 m, 6 cm) piece
- water in large container
- scissors
- clothespins or large paper clips

variation 2:
- poster board cut in strips
  - 1" (2.5 cm) strips;
    - cut four 20" (51 cm) strips
    - and two 15" (38 cm) strips
  - 1/2" (1.25 cm) strips; cut a total of
  - 12 feet in length
- yarn or string
- transparent tape
- scissors
- clothespins or large paper clips

▶ Steps to Follow

1. Lay the four 20" (51 cm) pieces side by side with 1/2" (1.25 cm) space between each.

2. Connect the four pieces by weaving the round reed (or yarn) back and forth across the center of the pieces four times. Cut the round reed (or yarn) and secure the ends by tucking them under the weaving or tying them.

3. If using reeds, soak them for at least fifteen minutes at this point.

4. Form the 4 pieces into the basket shape by folding in half. The woven part will be the base. The free ends will form the warp or spokes of the basket.

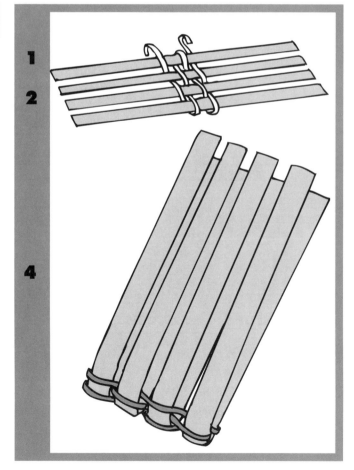

5. Cut one piece down its center on **one** side of the basket base to form two spokes. (You need an odd number of spokes for weaving.)

6. Using the 1/4" (.6 cm) reed (or 1/2" poster board strips) start weaving the weft. Start near the sewn base and go over and under the spokes around the basket. Continue to weave, working your way up the basket. If using reed, overlap each new piece of reed on the inside of the basket; poster board strips should be overlapped and taped. When you have 3" (7.5 cm) left on the warp spokes, stop weaving. Trim the ends of the "over" spokes to a point.

7. Fold the pointed spokes to the inside, tucking them behind the weft reed. Cut the "under" spokes even with the top of the basket.

8. Cut two 1" (2.5 cm) strips to fit the circumference of the top edge of the basket. Place one strip inside and one strip outside. Hold the strips in place with clothespins or large paper clips.

9. Using 1/4" (.6 cm) round reed (or yarn), attach the rim pieces to the basket. "Sew" over the top of the inside and outside rim and through each opening between the spokes. Continue around the rim. Secure the ends.

10. Optional: Add a loop of 1/4" (.6 cm) reed (or yarn) for hanging the basket.

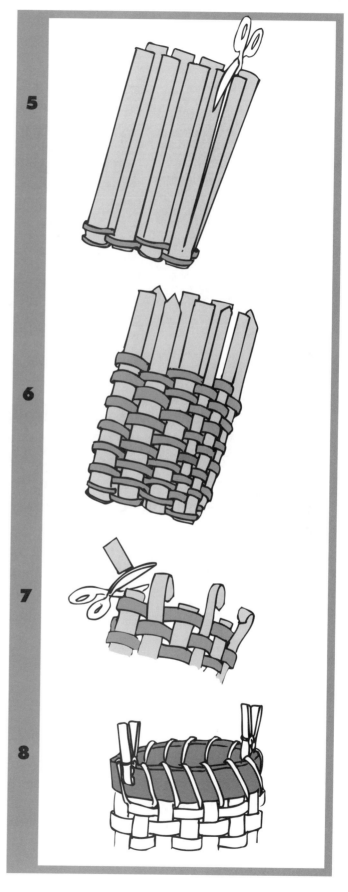

Clay Bead Necklace
Kenya

Beads are worn throughout Africa. Their design, patterns, and colors express positions in society, religion, politics, and style. Some of the beads used by the African people were carved from animal horns and tusks, while others were made of clay.

Traditionally beads were used in many ways, particularly in intricate hair braids, necklaces, and earrings.

Literature Connections

The Honey Hunters by Francesca Martin; Candlewick Press, 1992.
How Giraffe Got Such A Long Neck by Michael Rosen; Dial Books for Young Readers, 1993.
How the Ostrich Got Its Long Neck retold by Verna Aardema; Scholastic, 1995.
Inkishu by Kiol wa Mbugua; Jacaranda Designs Inc., 1994.
Little Big Ears, the Story of Eli by Cynthia Moss; Simon & Schuster, 1997.

Make a Clay Bead Necklace

▶ Materials

For the clay:
- flour
- salt
- water
- measuring cup
- bowl

For the necklace:
- wooden skewer
- sharp pencil or dowel
- cookie sheet
- acrylic paints
- waxed paper
- puff paint
- clear shellac (glossy)
- brushes
- 24" (61 cm) length of colored string or heavy thread
- small plastic beads (optional)

▶ Steps to Follow

Making the Clay
(enough for one necklace)

1. Dissolve one cup (200 g) of salt in one cup (240 ml) of warm water.

2. Stir in two cups (250 g) of flour.

3. Stir and knead until the dough is soft and pliable (about five minutes).

4. Keep dough in a sealed plastic bag until ready for use.

Making the Bead Necklace

1. Form small balls and other shapes out of clay. They should be about 1" (2.5 cm) high. Make at least twenty.

2. Push a skewer through the center of each ball to make a hole for stringing. Enlarge the hole by pushing a pencil or dowel through. The holes tend to close when baking if you don't make them big enough.

3. Place the beads one inch apart on a cookie sheet. Bake at 325° for 15 to 20 minutes or until they are lightly browned.

4. Paint the beads a solid color with acrylic paints.* Set the beads on waxed paper to dry. Then decorate them with contrasting colors and let dry again.

5. Shellac the dried beads. Several coats will make the beads shinier. Let beads dry between coats. They should dry overnight before stringing.

6. String the beads by threading them on the colored string or thread. Small plastic beads placed between the clay beads make good spacers. Tie a double knot to secure the ends.

Painting will be easier if you perch the beads on a pencil.

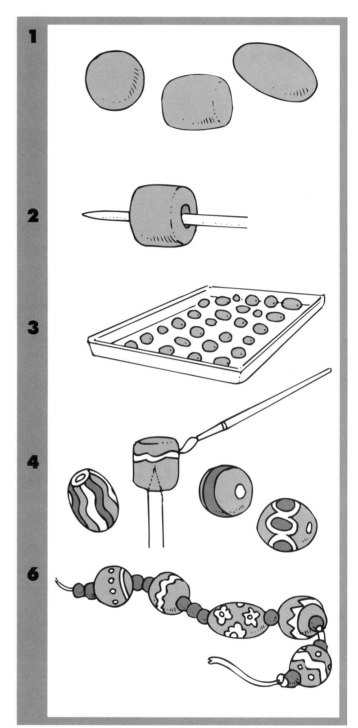

▶ **Suggestions for Bead Designs**

Nigerians are skilled metalworkers. They cast bronze sculptures and tiny pieces to be worn as jewelry. They also make decorative panels from hammered sheet metal.

Literature Connections

The Flying Tortoise: An Igbo Tale retold by Tololwa M. Mollel; Clarion Books, 1994.
Nigeria: One Nation, Many Cultures by Hassan Adeeb and Bonnetta Adeeb; Benchmark Books, 1996.
Why the Sun and Moon Live in the Sky by Niki Daly; Lothrop, Lee & Shepard Books, 1995.

Make a Hammered Metal Design

▶ **Steps to Follow**

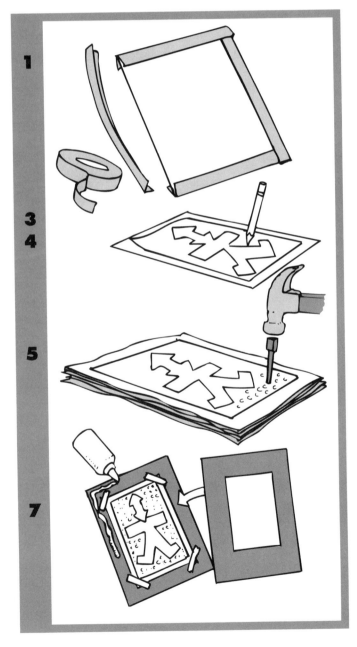

1. After cutting the sheet aluminum to size with scissors, tape the edges of the sheet aluminum rectangle to protect your fingers.

2. Choose one of the designs on pages 9 and 10 or draw one of your own.

3. Center the design on the metal rectangle and trace over all the lines. Press hard enough to transfer the lines to the metal.

4. Remove the paper and go over the lines with a sharp pencil.

5. Hammer the background using the nail set. Pack the marks close together to make an even pattern. Hint: Put the aluminum rectangle on the magazine before pounding. The magazine will cushion the strokes and absorb some of the noise.

6. When you have finished hammering, carefully flatten the rectangle.

7. Cut a rectangle out of the center of one of the poster board rectangles to create a frame. Secure the decorative panel to the back piece of the frame with tape. Glue the two pieces of poster board together.

9

Folk Art Projects•Around the World EMC 721

A Do Mask
Western Africa

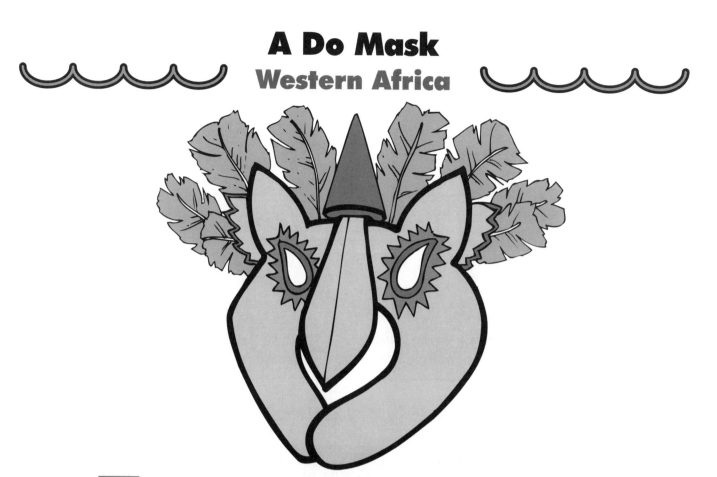

The Bobo tribesmen of Western Africa wear masks during their dance ceremonies that represent their guardian spirit Do. The horn on the front of the mask is used to spear evil spirits. According to legend, when all the dancers wearing the masks have finished the ceremony, the evil spirits are all securely held on the horn and cannot cause any more trouble. Peace then returns to the tribe.

Literature Connections

Emeka's Gift by Ifeoma Onyefulu; Cobblehill Books, 1995.
Gollo and the Lion by Eric Oyono; Hyperion Books for Children, 1994.
The Hunterman and the Crocodile retold by Baba Wague Diakite; Scholastic, 1997.
Koi and the Kola Nuts by Brian Gleeson; Rabbit Ears Books, 1992.
The Leopard's Drum by Jessica Souhame; Little, Brown, 1995.
Misoso retold by Verna Aardema; Alfred A. Knopf, 1994.
Tabu and the Dancing Elephants retold by Rene Deetlefs; Dutton Children's Books, 1995.
Too Much Talk by Angela Shelf Medeavis; Candlewick Press, 1995.
Too Much Talk by Jessica Souhami; Little, Brown, 1995.
Traveling to Tonda by Verna Aardema; Alfred A. Knopf, 1991.

Make a Do Mask

▶ **Materials**

- pattern on page 13
- 9" x 12" (23 x 30.5 cm) brightly colored construction paper
- 8" x 5" (20 x 13 cm) construction paper of a contrasting color

- markers
- feathers
- raffia
- stapler
- scissors
- glue or tape

▶ **Steps to Follow**

1. Fold the larger piece of construction paper in half the long way. Lay the main mask pattern on the fold and cut out the mask.

2. Cut the horn from the smaller piece of construction paper.

3. Use felt-tip markers to decorate the mask.

4. Cut out eyes. Fold the nose down. Reverse the fold in the nose to create dimension.

5. Form a cone out of the horn. Overlap so that the tabs line up. Staple to hold the cone together. Glue or tape the narrow part of cone.

6. Turn the mask wrong side up with the nose extended. Staple the horn as shown.

7. Fold the nose and horn down.

8. Overlap the two bottom edges of the mask and glue together to add dimension.

9. Add feathers and raffia to trim the mask.

1
2

4

5

6

8

9

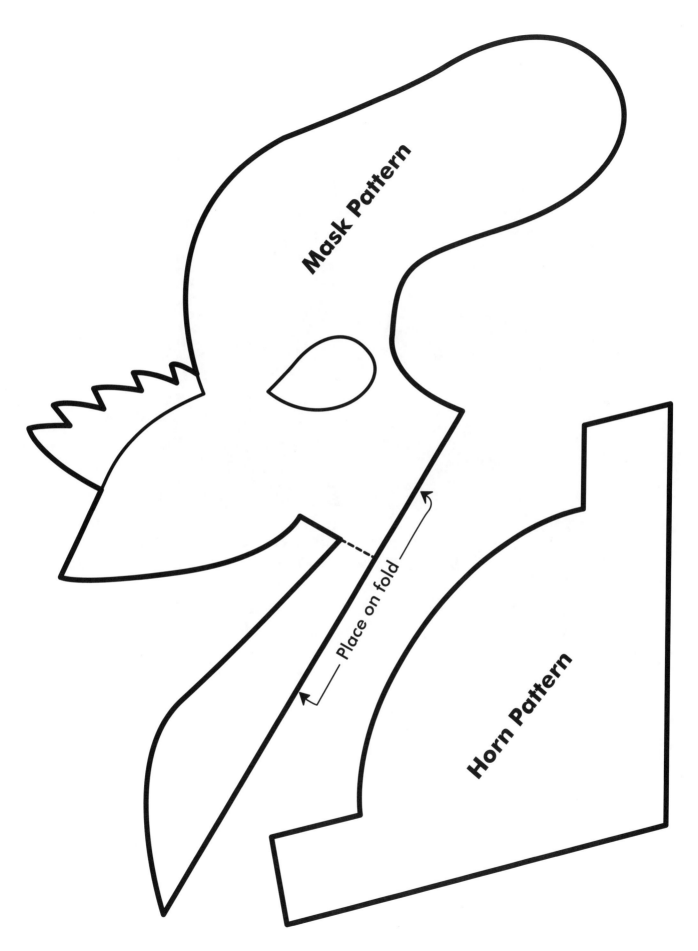

Mask Pattern

Horn Pattern

Place on fold

Folk Art Projects•Around the World EMC 721

Ancient Colombian artists created sculptures by soldering thick gold wire to a background made from a flat sheet of gold. Modern artists, like Pablo Picasso, imitated this style and technique in their work.

This sculpture substitutes cardboard and string for gold.

Literature Connections

Colombia by Marion Morrison; Children's Press, 1990.
Colombia - in Pictures; Lerner Publications Co., 1990.
The Money People by Eric Metaxas; Simon & Schuster, 1995.
Ransom of the River Dolphin by Sarita Kendall; Lerner Publications Co., 1993.

Make a Raised Line Sculpture

▶ Materials

- patterns on page 16
- lightweight cardboard (poster board, cereal box, tag board) sized to fit pattern
- carbon paper
- black poster board

- cotton macrame cord or string - bendable, but not too thin to handle
- gold spray paint
- scissors
- white glue

▶ Steps to Follow

1. Transfer the pattern of your choice to the cardboard using carbon paper or tracing with pencil, pressing hard enough to make an impression on the cardboard.

2. Cut out the outline shape.

3. Glue cord around the outline and over the design lines.

4. When the glue is dry, paint the design with gold paint. This may take two coats. Wait for the first coat to dry before applying the second coat.

5. Mount your sculpture on a piece of black posterboard cut to an appropriate size.

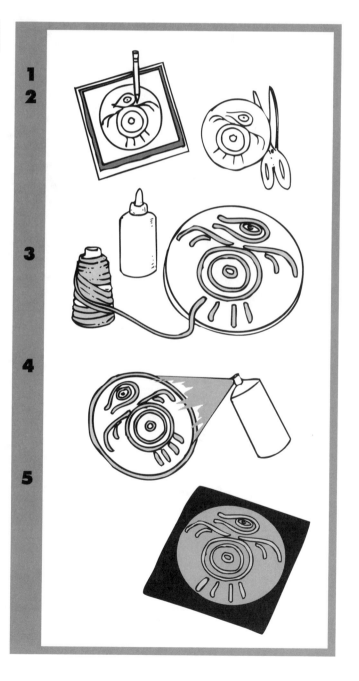

Folk Art Projects•Around the World EMC 721

Migajon
Ecuador

Migajon is a clay made from bread. It originated in Ecuador and is used throughout Central and South America today to make tiny toys and decorations.

Literature Connections

Ecuador by Erin L. Foley; Cavendish, 1995.
Headhunters and Hummingbirds by Robert McCracken; Walker, 1987.
Ecuador by Connie Bickman; Abdo & Daughters, 1996.
Ecuador by Emilie Lepthien; Children's Press, 1986.
Ecuador - in Pictures; Lerner Publications Co., 1994.
The Waorani by Alexandra Siy; Dillon Press, 1993.

Make Migajon Figures

▶ **Materials**

- two slices of white bread
- two tablespoons (30 ml) white glue
- acrylic paints
- glossy acrylic spray finish

▶ **Steps to Follow**

1. Trim the crust from the bread and tear the bread into tiny pieces.

2. Using your hands, mix the white glue into the bread. It will be very sticky at first, but will become clay-like as you knead it.

3. Form 1" (2.5 cm) balls of clay. Shape the clay into tiny animal figures or dishes. The animal shapes do not need to be very precise. Painting will add sufficient details.

4. Let the sculptures air dry or bake them in the oven. Keep the temperature set between 200° and 300° and check the sculptures regularly. The size and thickness of each piece will determine its baking time.

5. Paint the pieces with acrylic paints.

6. Spray each piece with a coat of glossy acrylic finish.

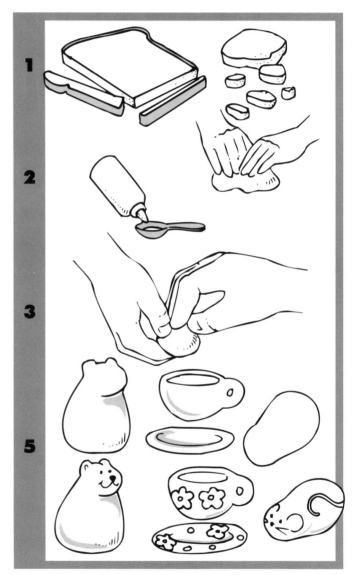

▶ **Hints**

1. Migajon can be tinted with food coloring before it is modeled.

2. If you use wheat bread or bread with whole grains you will make a clay with a darker, bumpy texture.

Beaded Bowl
Mexico

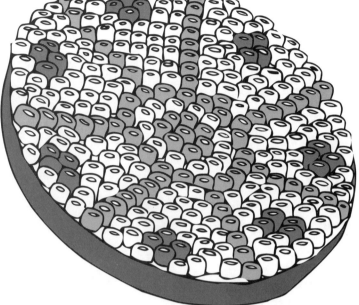

The Huichol Indians of Mexico make elaborate beaded bowls. Long ago, they coated the inside of dried half gourds with beeswax and formed symbolic pictures with seeds, kernels of corn, minute pebbles, shells, fluffy feathers, and white wads of cotton.

When the Spanish brought glass beads to Mexico, the Huichol people began using the beads to decorate their bowls. Picking up the tiny beads one by one on the point of a thorn or needle and pressing them into the soft wax, the artists created magical designs.

Literature Connections

De Colores selected by José-Luis Orozco; Dutton Children's Book, 1994.
Diego by Jeanette Winter; Dragonfly Books, 1991
Dragonfly's Tail retold by Kristina Rodanas; Clarion Books, 1991.

Make a Beaded Bowl

▶ Materials

- patterns on page 21
- 3"—3 1/2" (7.5—9 cm) dish (a jar lid or plastic plant-pot saucer work well)
- modeling clay
- map pin

- small beads or salad macaroni dyed in bright colors (Note: to dye macaroni, mix food coloring and rubbing alcohol in a zippered plastic bag and add macaroni.)

▶ Steps to Follow

1. Place a flat ball of plastic clay in the lid and smooth it up the sides and over the rim. Make an even coating about 1/4" (.6 cm) deep.

2. Lay your pattern from page 21 over the clay and transfer it by pricking through the pattern with the pin.

3. To place the beads, pick up each bead on the pin, stick the pin in position, and slide the bead down into place. Press gently to set the bead in place. Place beads tightly together in even rows with the holes all facing upward. To fill awkward spaces, beads can be placed sideways.

▶ Hints

You may enlarge the patterns on page 21 on a copy machine. The size that you choose needs to match your choice of bead. Colored macaroni will require a much larger pattern than seed beads will.

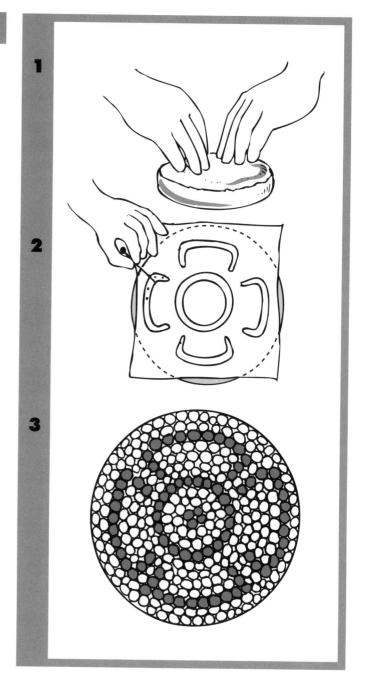

Folk Art Projects•Around the World EMC 721

Mask
Peru

The mask that inspired the pattern on page 24 was made in Peru sometime between 1200 and 1400. It was made of gold and decorated with brightly colored paint. The small pieces of gold that were hung from the mask jingled when the mask was moved.

Literature Connections

Chaska and the Golden Doll by Ellen Alexander; Arcade, 1994.
Miro in the Kingdom of the Sun by Jane Kurtz; Houghton Mifflin, 1996.
Peru by Emilie Ulepthien; Children's Press, 1992.

Make a Peruvian Mask

▶ Materials

- pattern on page 24
- file folder
- two beads (1/2" to 3/4" [1.25 - 2 cm] diameter)
- poster paint
- wide tip black marking pen
- scraps of foil paper or thin sheet aluminum (found at craft stores)
- two 1" (2.5 cm) pieces of broomstraw, or toothpicks with pointed ends snipped off
- thread
- needle
- hole punch
- tape
- scissors, craft knife
- glue

▶ Steps to Follow

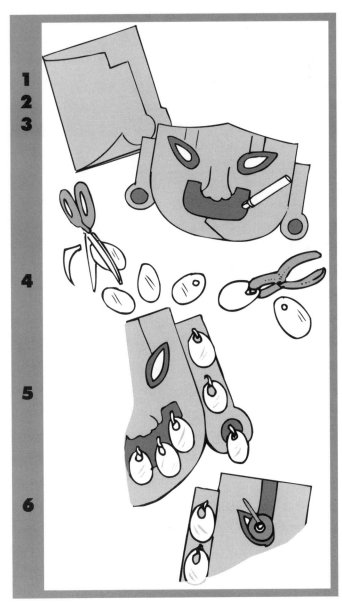

1. Trace the pattern on the file folder. Make sure that the fold line is positioned on the fold of the file folder.

2. Cut out the mask. Do not cut the fold.

3. Draw details with black marker and paint the mask form with poster paint. Dry completely. Retrace outlines with black marker.

4. Cut decorative shapes from the foil or sheet aluminum. Use a hole punch to make holes in foil shapes.

5. Attach foil shapes with thread so that they will move when the mask is moved. (Thread the needle and push the thread through the mask in places where you want to attach the foil shapes. Tie the thread to the shapes on the front of the mask. Tape the thread down on the back side.

6. Glue a bead in the center of each eye. Glue the broomstraw or toothpick piece in the center of each bead.

7. Add dimension to the mask:

   - Cut a small slit at the base of the chin and overlap the two sides to give the mask dimension.

   - Cut around the nose using a craft knife and bend the nose outward.

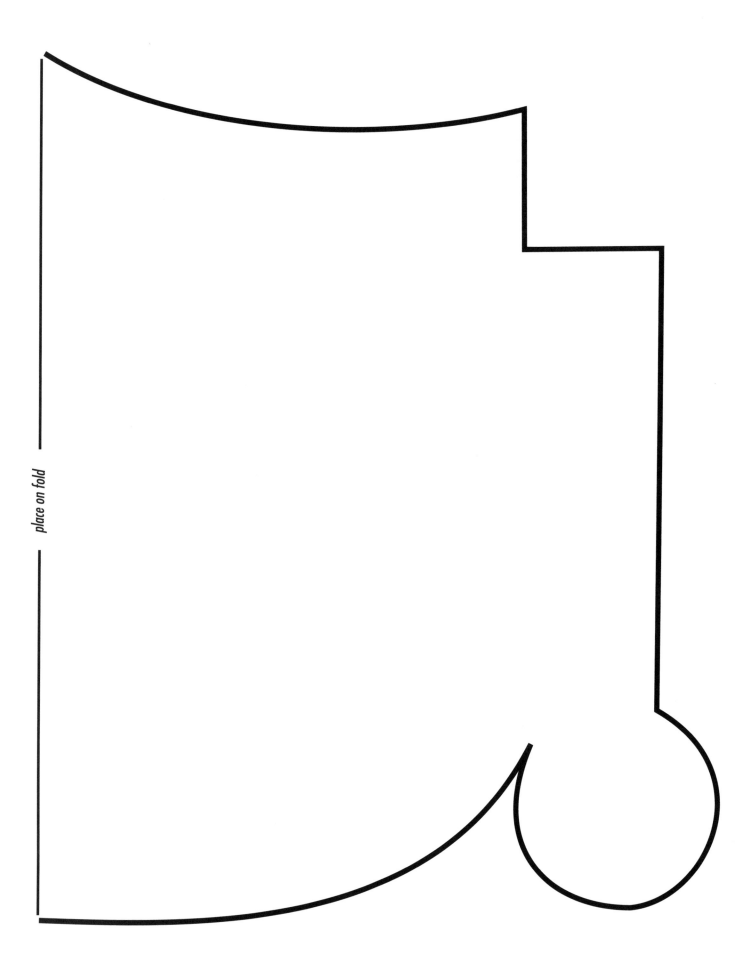

place on fold

24

Aboriginal Bark Pictures
Australia

The paper bark tree of Australia has soft, pliable bark that can be pulled off in large sheets. The Aborigines used these bark sheets for paintings. They painted with paints made from natural clays. They ground the clay up into a fine powder and then added animal fat for consistency, and blood or plant juices for color. Twigs, feathers, and fingers were used as paintbrushes.

Aborigines painted the things that they knew. Some designs were for beauty and some had special meanings. Most of the pictures tell stories. Designs in paintings and sculptures were often composed of complex combinations of dots, circles, semicircles, and diagonal lines. They also used the "X-ray" style, in which internal organs were shown.

Literature Connections

Dreamtime by Oodgeroo; Lothrop, Lee & Shepard Books, 1993.
Going for Oysters by Jeanie Adams; A. Whitman, 1994.
Rainbow Bird by Eric Maddern; Little, Brown, 1993.
The Singing Snake by Stefan Czernecki and Timothy Rhodes; Hyperion Books for Children, 1993.

Make Bark Pictures

▶ **Materials**

- templates made from patterns on page 27 traced on cardboard (optional)
- brown wrapping paper or grocery bag
- construction paper
- crayons and markers
- pictures of Australian animals for reference
- pieces of wood with a pronounced grain

▶ **Steps to Follow**

1. Tear the edges of a piece of brown wrapping paper or a large brown grocery bag. This rough edged paper will be your bark.

2. Lay the torn paper over the wood and rub a dark brown or black crayon over the paper. Pick up as much of the pattern of the wood grain as possible. This is called a relief print.

3. Using crayons or markers draw a simple Australian animal on the bark print (or use templates on page 27). Divide animal into a number of design areas. Fill in each area with lines and dots.

4. Glue the finished bark drawing onto a larger piece of construction paper.

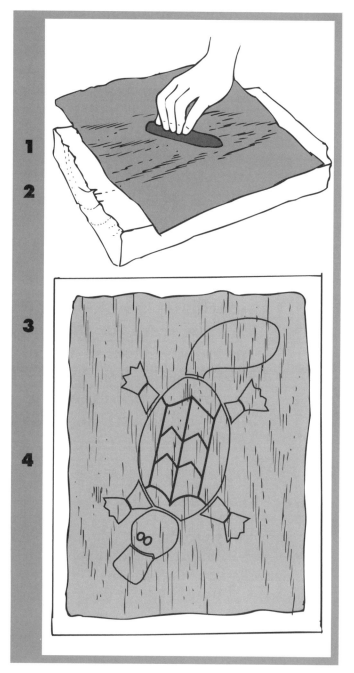

If your students need larger figures, enlarge these patterns with your copier before making templates.

Folk Art Projects•Around the World EMC 721

Palm Leaf Fans
China

In China, the lower part of a broad palm leaf was used as a fan. The edges were bound with strips of reed and the leaf stem became the handle. The leaves were painted with beautiful designs.

The stencil for this fan is a copy of a thirteenth-century Chinese building called a drum tower. These towers were like town gates. People had to pass through them to enter the town. A drummer in the tower warned the town if intruders tried to enter.

Literature Connections

China: Old Ways Meet New by Deborah Kent; Benchmark Books, 1996.
The Emperor and the Nightingale by Hans Christian Anderson; Simon & Schuster, 1995.
The Fourth Question retold by Rosalind C. Wang; Holiday House, 1991.
Land of Yesterday, Land of Tomorrow by Paul, David, and Peter Conklin; Cobblehill Books, 1992.
Little Plum by Ed Young; Philomel Books, 1994.
The Magic Tapestry retold by Demi; Henry Holt; 1994.
The Shell Woman and the King by Laurence Yep; Dial Books for Young Readers, 1993.
The Sleeper by David Day; Ideals Children's Books, 1990.
The Stonecutter by Demi; Crown Publisher Inc., 1995.

Make Palm Leaf Fans

▶ Materials

- patterns on page 31
- white poster board
- two tongue depressors per fan
- red and black tempera or acrylic paints
- black wide tip marker
- red string or heavy crochet thread

- 5" x 6" (13 x 15 cm) piece of file folder
- 3" x 2" (7.5 x 5 cm) piece of file folder
- sponge
- masking tape
- scissors
- craft knife (adult use only)
- spray gloss finish

▶ Steps to Follow

1. Cut the palm leaf shape out of the posterboard using the pattern provided.

2. Sandwich the "leaf" between two tongue depressors as shown. Glue the sticks in place.

3. Place the stencil of the drum tower (see directions on page 30 for making the stencil) in the center of the "palm leaf." Hold it in place with tiny pieces of masking tape.

4. Dip a sponge into a puddle of thick red paint. Press the sponge on a piece of paper towel to remove excess paint. Then fill in the openings of the stencil with the sponge. Press the sponge down and lift; don't move the sponge around. Redip sponge in paint as needed.

5. Remove the stencil carefully. If desired, stencil the other side after the paint has dried.

6. When the drum tower is dry, use black paint or marker to add a curved area at the base of the fan and a border around the edge. Paint the handle black. Let the paint dry.

7. Spray the fan with a glossy finish. Allow to dry.

8. Wrap the handle with the red string or thread. To begin, tape the end of the thread to the handle. Keep the wrapping close together so that the handle is covered by the thread. Tie the end.

9. Make a tassel as follows:

   a. Wrap string or thread many times around the short direction of the smaller piece of file folder.

   b. Cut a 6" (15 cm) piece of string or thread and slip it under one end of the wrapped strands. Tie a knot.

   c. Cut the other end of the wrapped strands and slip the tassel off the cardboard.

   d. Tie a short piece of string/thread around the tassel about 1/3 of the way down.

   e. Tie the tassel to the handle by wrapping the loose string around and through a strand of the handle wrapping.

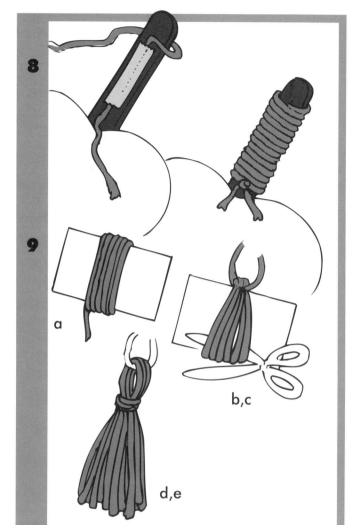

▶ Drum Tower Stencil

1. Transfer the drum tower pattern to the larger piece of file folder by using carbon paper or tracing the outline with a pencil, pressing hard enough to make an impression on the file folder.

2. Using the craft knife, cut out the areas of the drum tower. Make several stencils for students to share.

 Folk Art Projects•Around the World EMC 721

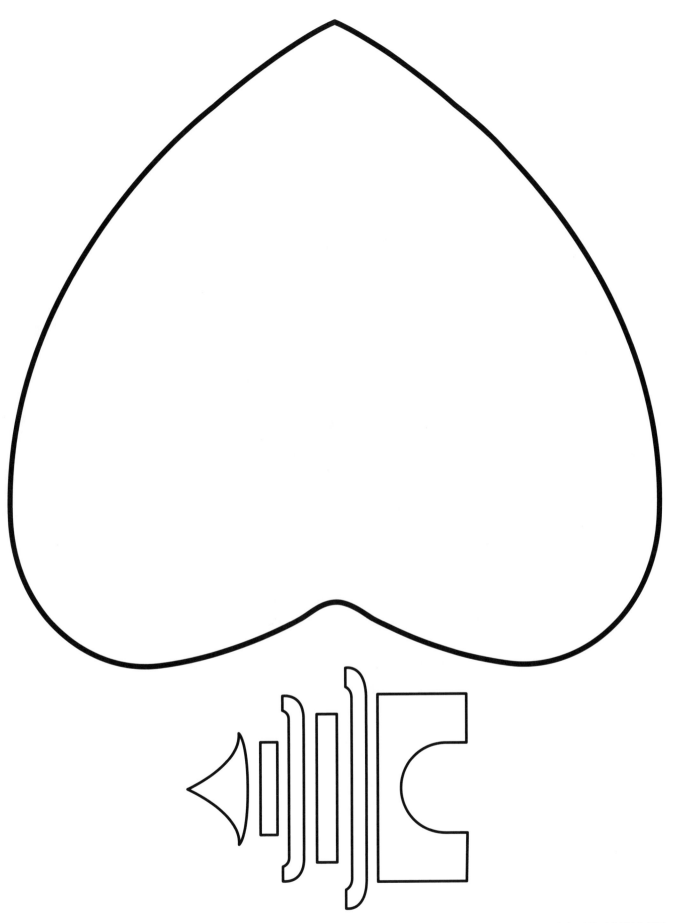

31

Torans
India

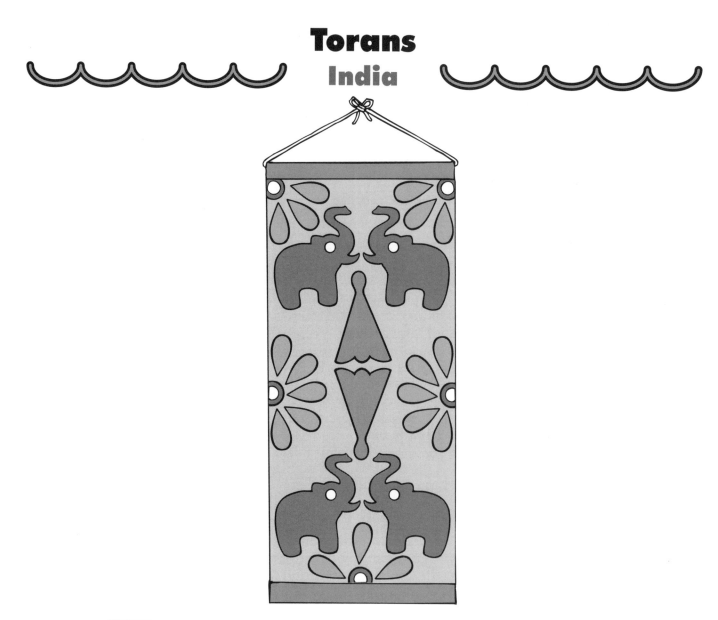

The Toran is a traditional hanging made in India. It is made in a square or a rectangle and is decorated with all types of embroidered animals, flowers, and other motifs set off by tiny mirrors that are sewed into the design.

Literature Connections

The Gifts of Wali Dad retold by Aaron Shepard; Atheneum Books, 1995.
In the Heat of the Village by Barbara Bash; Sierra Club Books, 1996.
In the Village of the Elephants by Jeremy Schmidt; Walker, 1994.
The Very Hungry Lion by Gita Wolf; Annick, 1996.

Make a Toran

► **Materials**

- patterns on page 35
- brightly colored felt
    - 11 1/2" x 4 1/2" (30 x 11.5 cm)
    - 1" x 4 1/2" (2.5 x 11.5 cm) of a contrasting color
    - 2" x 4 1/2" (5 x 11.5 cm) of a contrasting color
    - felt scraps in several colors

- five small circular mirrors (found in craft stores)
  or five 5/8" (1.5 cm) circles cut from an aluminum foil baking pan
- 4 1/2" (11.5 cm) piece of plastic drinking straw
- 15" (38 cm) piece of yarn, jute, or string
- white glue or hot glue gun
- scissors

► **Steps to Follow**

1. Cut felt scraps into flower and animal shapes. Use the patterns on page 35 if you wish.

2. Lay the cut felt pieces on the large felt rectangle. Move the pieces around until you are happy with the design.

3. Decide where to put the tiny mirrors. Cut circular frames of felt for each mirror or cut a hole in a larger felt piece where the mirror will be, as with the eye of the figure on the example on page 32.

4. Glue the mirrors and the pieces of felt, one at a time, to the felt rectangle.

5. Glue the 1" (2.5 cm) strip of felt to the bottom of your toran.

6. Fold the 2" (5 cm) strip of felt in half and glue the open edges together forming a tube.

7. Slide the drinking straw through the tube and glue the tube to the top of your toran. Glue so that the glued edge is hidden by the top of the toran.

8. Thread the string through the straw and tie the two ends together.

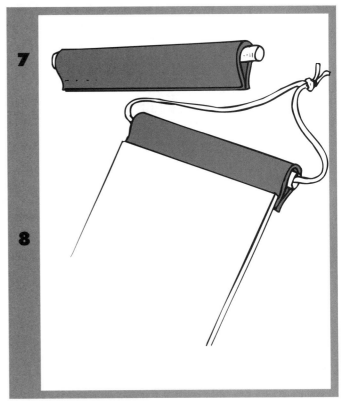

▶ **Optional**

You may want to use yarn to embroider around the felt shapes. The figures on Indian torans are decorated with embroidery and the mirrors are attached to the torans with a special framing stitch.

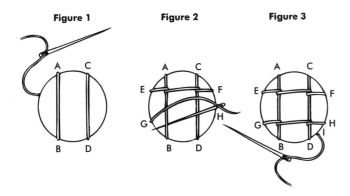

Figure 1   Figure 2   Figure 3

Here is another pattern option.

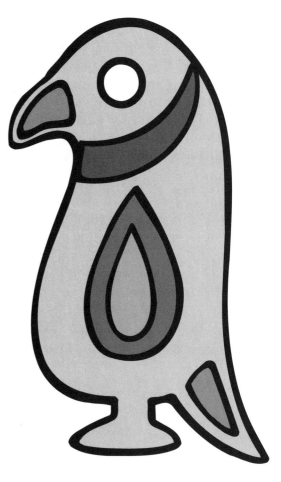

Folk Art Projects•Around the World EMC 721

Wayang Shadow Puppets
Indonesia

Shadow puppet shows are performed in Indonesia for special occasions and as entertainment. The person moving the puppets is called a dalang. (In Indonesia a dalang studies for about eight years and practices daily before he puts on a show.)

The puppets are made out of leather from young water buffalo hide. The puppets are cut with fine detail and sometimes painted. The dalang moves the puppets in front of a light to cast moving shadows on a screen.

The puppets are ugly and misshapen creatures since the Indonesians believe that it is sacrilegious to create anything resembling men and women.

Literature Connections

Indonesia by Sylvia McNair; Children's Press, 1993.
Small Deer's Magic Tricks by Betty Boegehold; Cowark, McGann & Geoghegan, 1977.

Make a Wayang Puppet

▶ **Materials**

- pattern on page 38
- 9" x 12" (23 x 30.5 cm) construction paper or lightweight poster board
- two pieces of thin doweling 12" (30.5 cm) and 20" (51 cm)
- three wooden skewers
- two small brads
- tape

▶ **Steps to Follow**

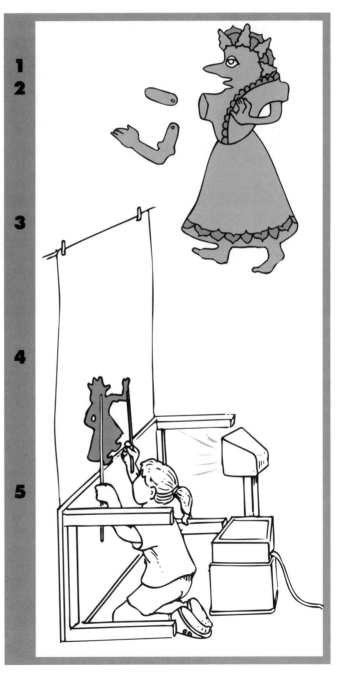

1. Reproduce the pattern on page 38 on the construction paper and trace it on the poster board.

2. Cut out the body and the two arm pieces.

3. Attach the arm pieces to the body with brads.

4. Decorate the puppet.

5. Tape the doweling to the back of the arm and body.

▶ **Hints**

Create a shadow theater with your overhead projector and a sheet.

>   Hang a sheet in an inside doorway or somewhere where there is space behind it.

- Turn a table on its side behind the sheet.
- Put a light source (an overhead projector with the light pointing forward works) in back of the sheet.

Puppeteers will sit on the floor behind the table but in front of the light. Adjust the distance between the light and the sheet so that the shadows of the puppets held up by the puppeteers show on the sheet.

The audience sits in front of the sheet.

Folk Art Projects•Around the World EMC 721

Mizuhiki
Japan

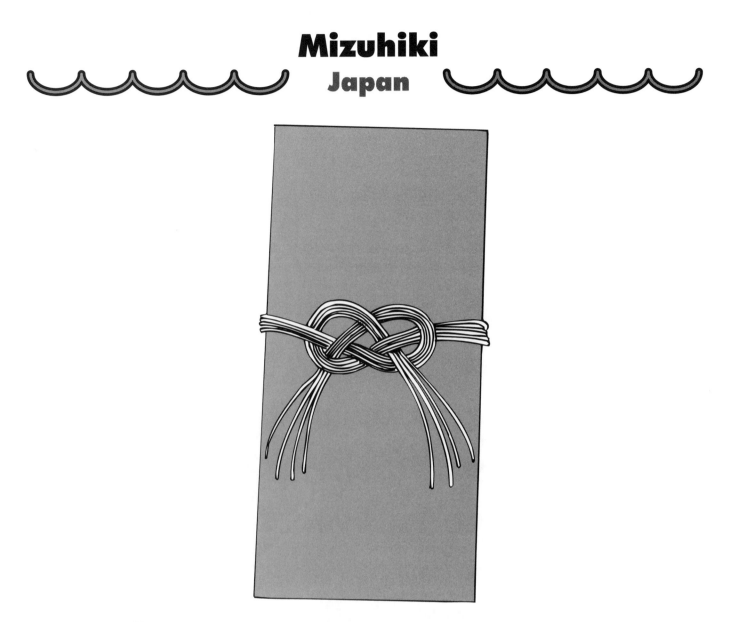

Traditional Japanese gifts are wrapped and tied with a bow made from thin colored cords. The cords are called mizuhiki (mee-zoo-HEE-key).

Literature Connections

Screen of Frogs retold by Sheila Hamanaka; Orchard Books, 1993.
The Snow Country Prince by Daisaku Ikeda; Alfred A. Knopf, 1990.
The Snow Wife by Robert D. San Souci; Dial Books for Young Readers, 1993.
Tsubu the Little Snail by Carol Ann Williams; Simon & Schuster, 1995.
(Also see page 42.)

Make Mizuhiki

▶ **Materials**

- four pieces of 30" (76 cm) thin colored cord (mizuhiki cords can be purchased at many art and craft supply stores, but thin cord sold for wrapping presents also works well)

- patterns on page 41 (optional)
- 4" x 8" (10 cm x 19 cm) poster board
- 6" x 10" poster board (optional)

▶ **Steps to Follow**

1. Lay the four cords side by side across the center of the back side of the poster board. Tape them in the center.

2. Turn the poster board rectangle over. The cords should extend to the right and left of the rectangle.

3. Wrap the cords across the top of the rectangle as if you were going to tie them.

4. With the cords on the left, make a loop about 6" (15 cm) from the cut end. Make sure that the cords lay flat against the poster board.

5. Weave the cords on the right in and out of the first loop as shown.

6. Adjust the cords so that the strands lay flat and the loops are of uniform size. Trim the ends near the knot so that they are even.

7. Optional
   - Cut out a message from page 41 and glue it to the top of the poster board.
   - Mount the mizuhiki on a larger piece of poster board.

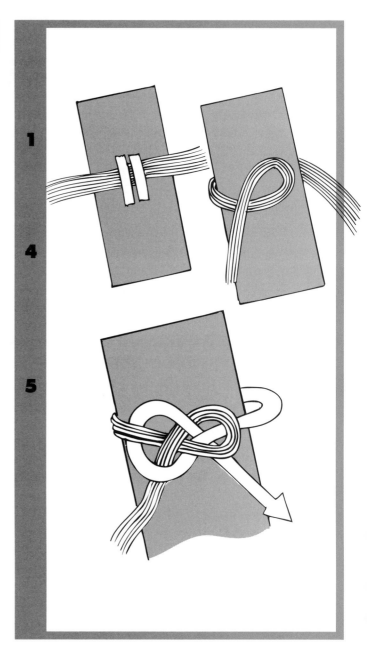

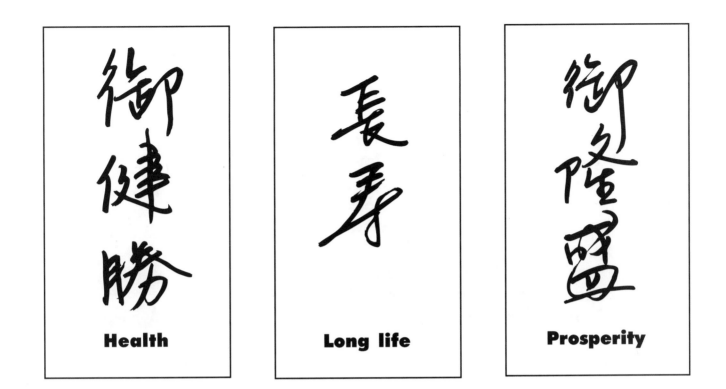

Health

Long life

Prosperity

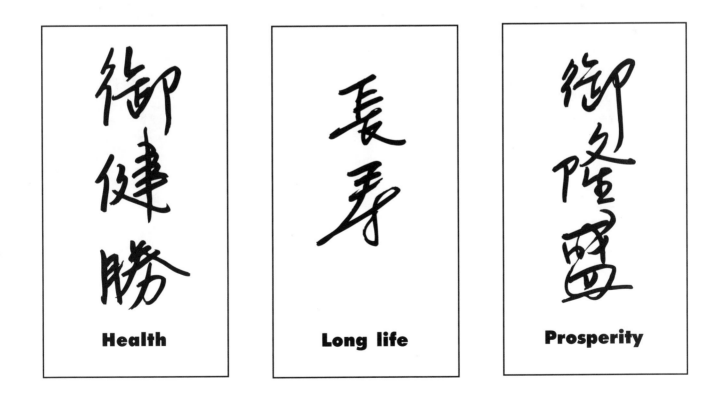

Health

Long life

Prosperity

Star Streamer
Japan

Tanabata (tah-nah-BAH-tah) is a popular Japanese festival. It is based on a story about a star princess who was a weaver. She fell in love with the cow-herd star. The two were so in love that they didn't do their work. The princess's father sent them to opposite ends of the Milky Way. They were allowed to meet just once a year on the seventh day of the seventh month. On that day they crossed the skies on a bridge made of birds.

To celebrate the holiday, Japanese children write poems on long strips of paper and tie them to branches of trees. Festive paper streamers representing the Milky Way decorate the streets. The streamers are made using origami paper-folding techniques.

Literature Connections

The Farmer and the Poor God retold by Ruth Wells; Simon & Schuster, 1996.
Jojofu by Michael P. Waite; Lothrop, Lee & Shepard Books, 1996.
Lily and the Wooden Bowl by Alan Schroeder; Doubleday Books for Young Readers, 1994.
Little Inchkin by Fiona French; Dial Books for Young Readers, 1994.
(Also see page 39.)

Make Star Streamers

▶ Materials

- squares of origami paper or gift wrap — 4 1/2" (11.5 cm)
- a stick about 2 feet (60 cm) long
- a needle with a large eye
- three 18" (45.5 cm) lengths of thin string
- beads or Cheerios

▶ Steps to Follow

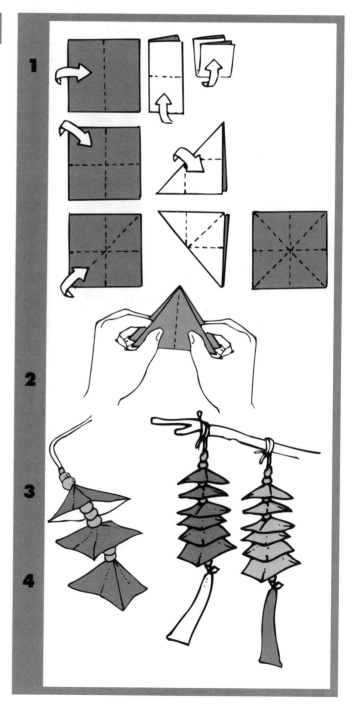

1. To make one paper triangle:
   - Fold the paper square (colored side in) in half to make a rectangle. (Crease all folds well.)
   - Fold the rectangle in half again to make a small square.
   - Unfold completely.
   - Fold in half diagonally.
   - Unfold and fold in half diagonally the other way.
   - Open the paper and lay it colored side up. If you have creased all folds well, the paper will be raised off the surface.
   - Take two adjacent corners and pull them together. Repeat with the opposite set of corners. You now have back-to-back triangles, or a star shape when opened slightly.
   Make 17 or more triangles.

2. Divide the paper triangles into three sets and string them on the pieces of string using the needle and thread. Put 3 beads or 6 Cheerios in between each triangle so that the triangles stay apart. Align the flaps of each triangle so that it fits into the slits of the triangle below it.

3. Tie the star strands to the stick.

4. Add a poem written on a long strip of paper to your stick.

A Thunderbolt
New Zealand

The Tohunga, a part of the Maori people in New Zealand, whirled a wooden paddle over their heads to frighten away the evil spirits that helped the God of Storms. During times of drought, they swung it round and round to summon the God of Rain. They called this paddle a Purerehua or Thunderbolt.

Children will love playing with this wonderful noisemaker.

Literature Connections

Land of the Long White Cloud by Kiri Te Kanawa; Arcade, 1989.
Kuma Is a Maori Girl by Dennis Hodgson; Hastings House, 1967.
New Zealand by Mary Virginia Fox; Children's Press, 1991.
Punga the Goddess of Ugly by Deborah Nourse Lattimore; Harcourt Brace Jovanovich, 1993.

Make a Thunderbolt

▶ Materials

- pattern on page 46
- 2 1/2" x 6" (6 x 15 cm) piece of 1/4" (6 mm) basswood (a heavy balsa-type wood)
- 1/2" (13 mm) dowel - 7" (18 cm) long

- coping saw or jig saw
- 1/8" drill bit
- 27" (68 cm) length of heavy twine
- sandpaper
- paint or markers

▶ Steps to Follow

1. Trace the pattern for the thunderbolt blade on the wood.

2. Cut out the blade using a coping saw or jig saw.

3. Use pattern to locate the position of the hole for the cord. Drill a 1/8" hole for the cord.

4. Sand edges and surfaces smooth. Round all of the corners.

5. Sketch and paint the design on the blade.

6. Apply a coat of shellac or vinyl sealer and allow the sealer to dry.

7. Fasten one end of the cord to the blade.

8. Drill a 1/8" hole in the dowel. Fasten the free end of the cord to the top of the dowel.

9. Playing with the thunderbolt:
   - Use the thunderbolt outdoors in a clear area.
   - Make sure that no one is close by.
   - Hold the handle in one hand, then swing the blade in a circle over your head, gradually increasing speed until your thunderbolt roars in the wind.

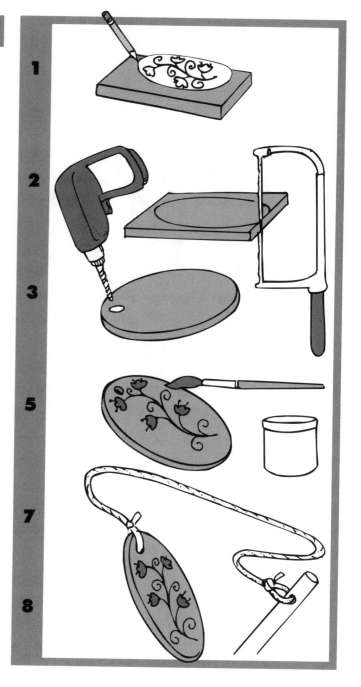

Folk Art Projects•Around the World EMC 721

In Southeast Asian countries, a person's signature is stamped instead of written, using a personal seal known as a chop. Chops can be made of many materials including gold, silver, copper, brass, steel, bronze, jade, and soapstone. The chop is inked and a print is made wherever a signature is required.

Literature Connections

The Golden Cup and Other Tales by Lynette Vuong; Lothrup, Lee & Shepard Books, 1993.
The Jade Stone adapted by Caryn Zacowitz; Holiday House, 1992.
Nine-In-One, Grr! Grr! by Blia Xiong; Children's Book Press, 1989.
Vietnam by Andrew Sech; Cavendish, 1994.

Make a Chop

▶ **Materials**

- art gum eraser
- craft knife
- sharp pencil

- stamp pad
- art gum eraser or rectangle cut from a Styrofoam® meat tray

▶ **Steps to Follow**

1. Write name or initials on a piece of scrap paper smaller than the eraser or the Styrofoam block.

2. Turn the scrap paper facedown on the eraser or Styrofoam. Trace over the lines. This will create small indentations in the chop to use as a pattern.

3. Remove the paper. Retrace the lines on the chop using the pencil or the craft knife. The letters will be written backwards.

4. Press the carved surface of the chop firmly on to an ink stamp pad.

5. Press the chop onto a paper to print the signature.

▶ **Hints**

1. If you are making a Styrofoam® chop you may want to mount the Styrofoam to a wooden block for easier printing. White craft glue will work for this.

2. Wash meat trays with soap and water before using. This will help the ink to adhere more easily.

3. Use name chops to sign books, paintings, creative writing projects, cards.

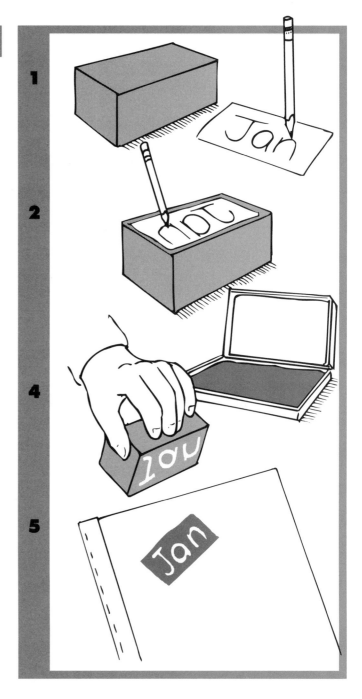

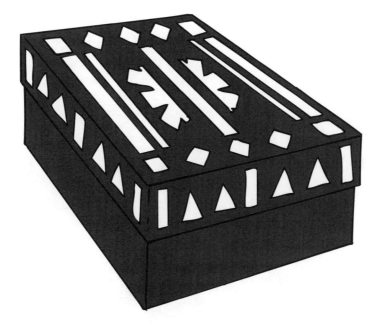

The straw designs of Belarus are made with flattened rye straw glued onto wood that has been dyed black. Solid areas are made from long strips of straw glued next to one another. Small squares, triangles, and thin strips are cut from the straw and glued to the wood to make village scenes, people, and animals.

Literature Connections

Belarus; Lerner Publications Co., 1993.
Belarus, Ukraine, and Moldova by Kelvin Gosnell; Millbrook Press, 1992.

Make "Straw" Designs

▶ **Steps to Follow**

1. Paint the box black. Let it dry completely.

2. Sketch designs on scratch paper until you find ones that please you. Use geometric shapes and lines.

3. Cut strips, triangles, and squares from the ribbon.

4. Glue the ribbon pieces in place to make the design on the black box. You may wish to put a design on several sides of the box.

5. Seal the complete box with a coat of polyurethane.

▶ **Hints**

1. Make an overhead transparency of the design samples on page 51 to give students an idea about design possibilities.

2. Keep a damp sponge handy for wiping off gluey fingers.

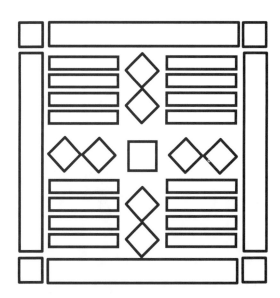

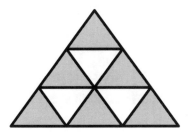

Paper Filigree
England

Filigree is any ornamental openwork with an intricate design. In English churches during the fifteenth century, designs were made by coiling narrow strips of paper and allowing them to spring open into various shapes. The monks used paper to copy the metal filigree designs on decorative screens and panels.

Later paper filigree became a craft for young ladies and a pastime for wartime prisoners. Boxes, chests, cabinets, trays, and picture frames were decorated with tiny paper coils.

When paper filigree was brought to America by the Colonists, it came to be known as quilling, since the tiny paper strips were often wrapped around quills.

Literature Connections

The Old Woman Who Lived in a Vinegar Bottle by Margaret Read MacDonald; August House Little Folk, 1995.
Tattercoats collected and edited by Joseph Jacobs; Putnam, 1989.
The True Adventure of Daniel Hall by Diane Stanley; Dial Books for Young Readers, 1995.
Duffy and the Devil by Harve Zemach; Farrar, Straus, Giroux, 1973.

Make Paper Filigree

► Materials

- 1/4" x 6" (6 mm x 15 cm) strips of lightweight paper, such as origami paper, in various colors
- 1/4" x 9" (6 mm x 23 cm) strips for fish outline

- toothpicks
- narrow skewer, toothpick, or knitting needle
- white glue
- 3" x 5" (7.5 x 13 cm) construction paper

► Steps to Follow

1. Make about 12 circular coils using 6" (15 cm) paper. For each coil:

   - Wrap a paper strip around a skewer.
   - Slide the coil off the skewer.
   - Let it uncoil a bit.
   - Glue the outside end to the coil.

2. Make the outside of the fish using 9" (23 cm) paper:

   - Fold a strip in half.
   - Curl each end to the outside wrapping it around the skewer several times.
   - Form the fish shape and glue the two ends together at the tail.

3. Fill the fish with circular coils. Glue the coils to the fish outline and to each other using the toothpick and white glue.

4. Let the fish dry.

5. Dip one side of fish in glue. Place on paper. Add a paper curl in each corner.

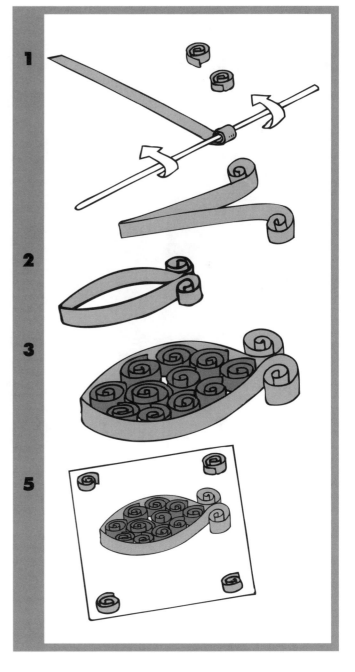

▶ Hints

1. The width of the strips can vary. Choose a size that is appropriate for your project. Traditionally filigree was worked with 1/8" (3 mm) strips. Strips over 1" (2.5 cm) wide tend to collapse.

2. A quilling tool can be made by cutting a small slit in the end of a dowel. The paper strips are slipped into the slit and can be rolled quickly.

3. When gluing the coils, use a toothpick dipped in glue. Stick the toothpick in a damp sponge between gluing to eliminate dripping glue.

4. A sheet of waxed paper makes an excellent working surface. The shapes being glued together will not stick to it.

▶ More Filigree

If your students are successful and enjoy the filigree work, let them experiment with their own designs using a variety of filigree shapes.

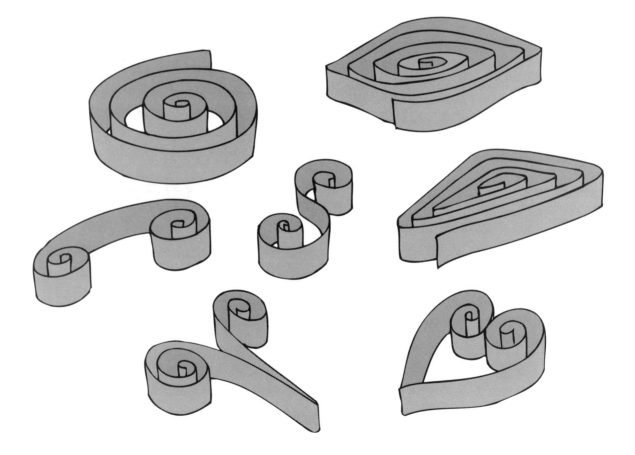

Scrimshaw
England

The art of scrimshaw was developed by American and British-American whalers in the early 1800s. The whalers carved an object from a piece of whalebone. The piece to be worked on was shaped with a saw or file and then smoothed and polished. Later designs were etched into the piece with a sharp instrument, usually a jackknife, and rubbed with a coloring to make the etchings stand out. The subjects of most scrimshaw were nautical in nature - sailing ships, whales, birds, etc.

Literature Connections

Whaling — Blow Ye Winds Westerly by Elizabeth Gemwang; Crowell, 1971.
Whaling Days by Carol Carrick; Clarion Books, 1993.

Make Scrimshaw

▶ Materials

- white pvc connector - 1 1/2" (3.8 cm) long, 1" (2.5 cm) in diameter
- etching nail (push nail through cork) 1"—1 1/2" (2.5—4 cm) piece of cork 2" (5 cm) long thin nail
- leather cord or shoestring
- permanent black marker
- fine steel wool

▶ Steps to Follow

1. Draw a design or picture on the pipe with pencil.

2. With etching nail, trace over the drawing to cut lines in the plastic.

3. Cover the images with black marker.

4. Buff the ink off the plastic with steel wool. The incised lines will remain black.

5. Put the cord through the pipe and the scrimshaw becomes a necklace or a key chain ornament.

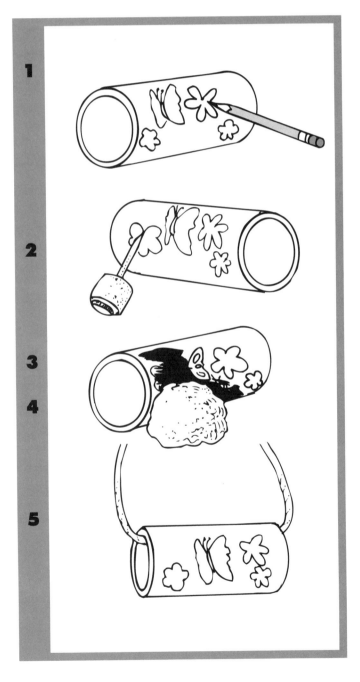

Fleur-de-lis Bowl
France

In eighteenth century France, small boxes and bowls made of papier-mâché were very popular. The symbol used to decorate this bowl is a stylized iris bloom called a fleur-de-lis. It was chosen by King Charles V to be the royal symbol. In France today the fleur-de-lis can be seen adorning buildings, china, and leather goods.

Literature Connections

Burgoo Stew by Susan Patron; Orchard Books, 1991.
France by Philippe Pierre; Gareth Stevens Children's Books, 1990.
Nekane, the Lamina and the Bear by Frank P. Araujo; Rayre Productions, 1993.
The King's Day by Aliki; Crowell, 1989.
Three Perfect Peaches by Cynthia De Felice and Mary De Marsh; Orchard Books, 1995.

Make a Fleur-de-lis Bowl

▶ Materials

- fleur-de-lis pattern on page 59, cut from tagboard
- small bowl
- dark blue tempera paint
- polymer medium (gloss) - can be purchased in jars at craft or art supply stores
- gold enamel paint

- fine point paintbrushes
- fine tip black markers, both washable and permanent
- sandpaper
- newspaper
- flour
- water
- white glue
- Vaseline®

▶ Steps to Follow

Papier-mâché preparation:

1. Tear or cut newspapers into strips, 1/2 inch wide and as long as the sheet of paper.

2. Mix a bowl of paste. Start with 1/2 cup of flour. Add 1/4 cup of water, stirring all the time so that the flour will not lump. When it is well mixed, add more water to make a thin paste. Add 1 tablespoon of white glue to the flour mixture. Stir until well mixed.

Making the bowl:

1. Turn the small bowl upside down on the working surface. It will be used as a mold. Cover the bowl with Vaseline®.

2. Pour the paste into a wide, shallow dish. Pull strips of paper through the paste and wrap them around the mold. Crisscross the strips in all directions and cover the bowl evenly. Build up a thickness of 1/4 inch all over the bowl.

3. If desired, pinch the papier-mâché around the rim as you would a pie crust to create a scalloped effect.

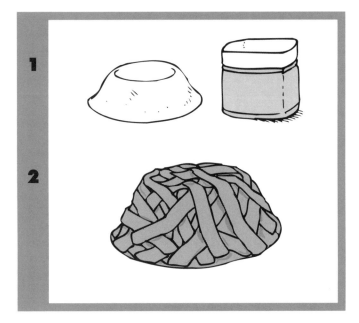

4. Let the papier-mâché dry until it is stiff enough to hold its shape. Remove from the bowl and turn it upright as it continues to dry. (If you let the papier-mâché dry too much while it remains on the overturned bowl, it will shrink tightly against the mold, making removal difficult.)

5. Dry the papier-mâché bowl completely.

Finishing the bowl:

1. Gently sandpaper the inside and outside of the bowl to smooth the surfaces.

2. Paint the outside surface of the bowl with two or three coats of blue paint. Let the surface dry between coats. Then turn the bowl right side up and apply two or three coats to the inside surface, drying between coats.

3. Apply one or two coats of the polymer medium to both the inside and outside surfaces of the bowl, drying between coats.

4. Place fleur-de-lis pattern in bottom of bowl and trace around with washable marker.

5. Paint fleur-de-lis with gold paint.

6. Decorate the top edge of the bowl with a band of gold paint.

7. When the gold paint is dry, go around the fleur-de-lis with the permanent marker.

8. Apply additional coats of the polymer gloss.

pattern

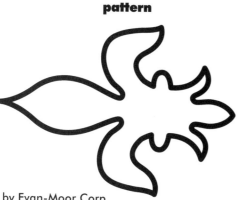

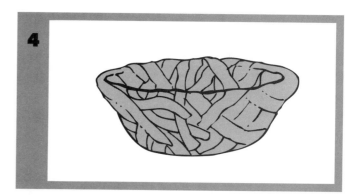

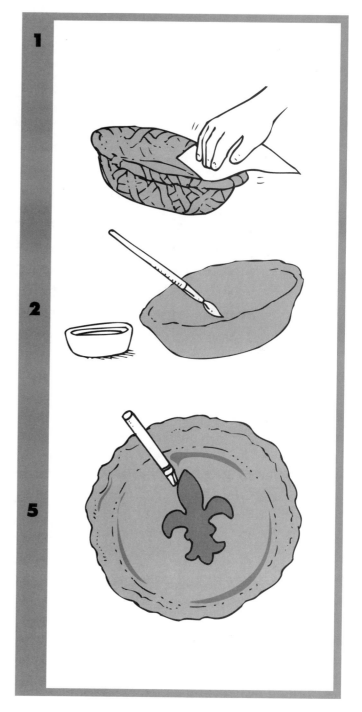

Schultute

Germany

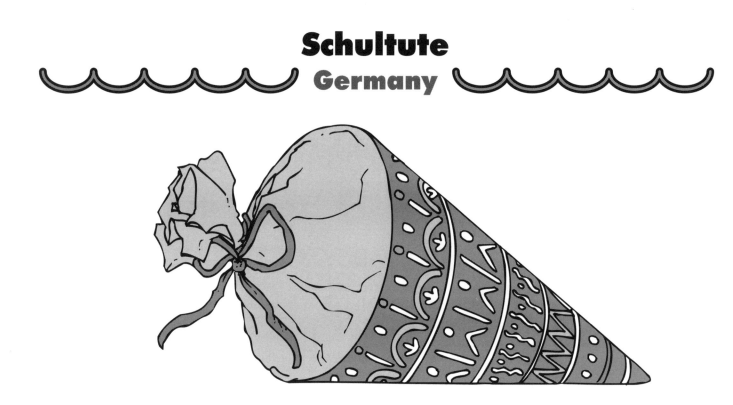

German children entering the first grade are given a gift on the first day of school. The large, decorated paper cone is called a Schultute (SHOOL-tur-tuh). It is filled with candy, pencils, and small gifts. The gift makes the scary first day of school a little easier.

In Germany the cones are usually purchased and then filled. Here are the directions to make your own cone.

Literature Connections

Around the Oak by Gerda Muller; Dutton Children's Books, 1994.
The Bear and the Bird King retold by Robert Byrd; Dutton Children's Books, 1994.
The Four Gallant Sisters by Eric Kimmel; Henry Holt, 1992.
The Goose Girl by Jacob and Wilhelm Grimm; North-South Books, 1988.
The Hero of Bremen by Margaret Hodges; Holiday House, 1993.
Iron John adapted by Eric A. Kimmel; Holiday House, 1994.
Kisses from Rosa by Petra Mathers; Alfred A. Knopf, 1995.
Rose Blanche by Roberto E. Innocenti; Creative Education, 1995.

Make a Schultute

▶ Materials

- 11" (28 cm) newspaper square
- 11" (28 cm) poster board square
- markers or "puff" paints
- 6" x 18" (15 x 45.5 cm) tissue paper
- stapler

- white glue
- tape
- scissors
- treats for stuffing the Schultute
- 12" (30 cm) ribbon or yarn

▶ Steps to Follow

1. Fold the newspaper square in half diagonally. Measure down the fold 4" (10 cm) and make a mark. Cut a curved line from the outer corner to the mark on the fold.

2. Use the newspaper template to cut the poster board square.

3. Decorate the poster board with markers and paint.

4. Roll the poster board into a cone shape. Staple and tape the edge.

5. Glue the tissue paper strip around the inside edge of the cone so that most of it sticks up above the cone.

5. Fill the cone with treats.

6. Gather the tissue paper together in the center and tie it closed with a ribbon.

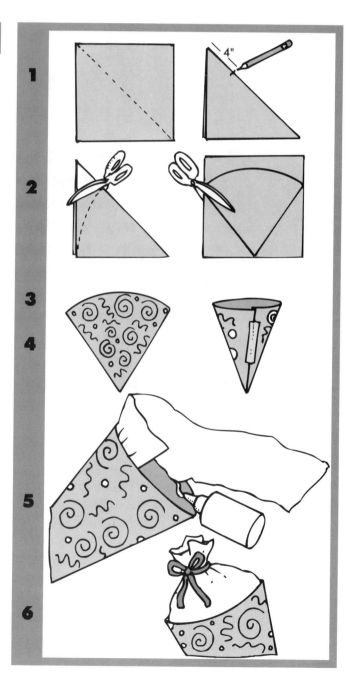

Mosaics
Greece

Mosaic is an art form where small pieces of cut stone or glass are embedded in a plaster bed. The art of mosaic was developed in Ancient Greece. As early as 500 B.C. mosaics made of small stones were used to decorate the floors of houses in Greece.

Later they decorated walls in houses, public buildings, and churches throughout Europe. The first mosaics were made out of white pebbles embedded in a background of black pebbles. Colorful pebbles, jewels, clay tiles, and glass were used during later times.

Literature Connections

Arion and the Dolphin by Vikram Seth; Dutton Children's Books, 1995.
The Eggs: A Greek Folktale retold by Aliki; HarperTrophy, 1994.
Greece by R. Conrad Stein; Children's Press, 1987.
Niki's Little Donkey by Coby Hol; North-South Books, 1993.
Persephone retold by Warwick Hutton; M.K. McElderry Books, 1994.
Theseus and the Minotaur by Leonard Everett Fisher; Holiday House, 1988.

Make a Dolphin Mosaic

▶ Materials

- pattern on page 64
- 9" x 12" (28 x 30.5 cm) white corrugated cardboard (or paint one side of regular cardboard)

- black beans
- white beans
- white rice
- white glue

▶ Steps to Follow

1. Cut out the pattern on page 64, and trace it onto the corrugated cardboard using a light pencil line. To transfer the areas within the outline, trace over the lines, press hard enough to leave an impression on the cardboard.

2. Cover a small area of the figure with glue. Put down beans around the outside of the glued area. Fill the area in with beans of the same color. Do one section at a time until the entire pattern is covered. Do not put down glue in a large area; it will dry too fast.

3. Create a decorative border for your mosaic using both black and white beans. Fill in the remaining background with rice.

4. Let the glue dry overnight. Spray the mosaic with clear acrylic fixer or paint it with a 1 to 3 mixture of white glue and water. Let the finish coat dry.

5. When you have finished, cover the mosaic with wax paper or aluminum foil. Then lay a heavy book on top to keep the cardboard from curling. Let the mosaic dry completely.

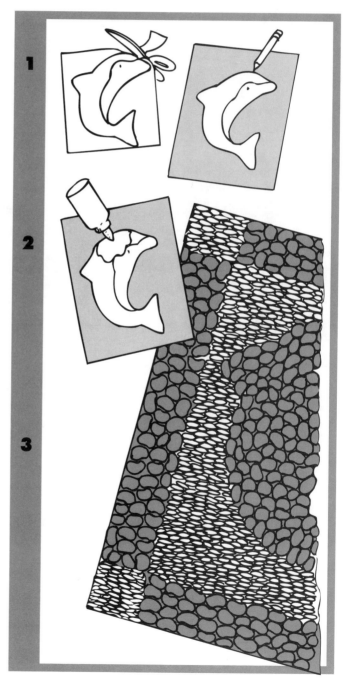

Folk Art Projects•Around the World EMC 721

Crois Bride
Ireland

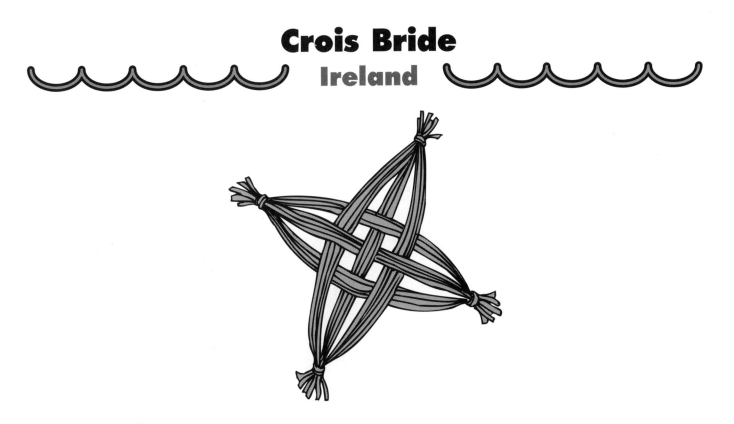

St. Brigid is the patron saint of the dairy and its cows. In Ireland barns and houses are often decorated with a crois Bride (cris breedge) or St. Brigid's cross. The cross was thought to protect the buildings from fire and other harm.

There are many different versions of the crois. Some are diamond-shaped, others look like pinwheels. The traditional crois is made from rushes. Irish school children might weave a crois Bride like the one in this project.

Hang your finished crois Bride over a doorway.

Literature Connections

Ireland by Patricia Marjorie Levy; Cavendish, 1994.
The Irish Cinderlad by Shirley Climo; HarperCollins, 1996.
The Irish Piper by Jim Latimer; Charles Scribner's Sons, 1991.
Jamie O'Rourke and the Big Potato by Tomie de Paola; Putnam, 1992.
Tales for the Telling by Edna O'Brien; Atheneum Books, 1986.

Make a Crois Bride

▶ Materials

- thin string - four 6" (15 cm) pieces
- raffia - a handful of 12" (30 cm) pieces

▶ Steps to Follow

1. Divide the raffia into two equal-sized bunches.

2. Wrap string several times around one end of each bunch. Tie the string.

3. Split each tied bunch of raffia into three sections.

4. Weave the three sections of one bunch under and over the sections of the other bunch another as shown.

5. Wrap and tie the loose ends with string.

6. Adjust the two bunches by moving them gently until you are happy with the crois.

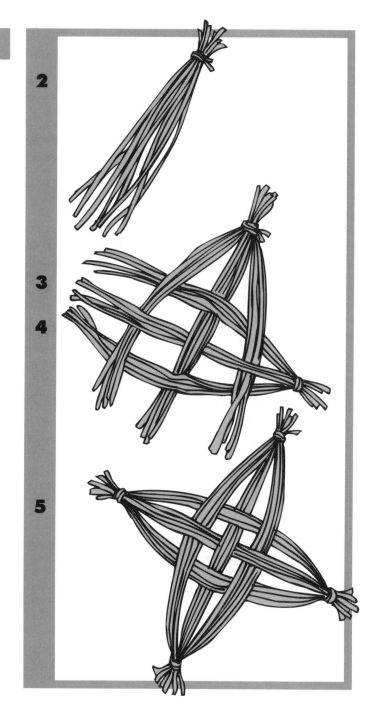

Wycinanki
Poland

Wycinanki (vi-chee-nan-kee) is the special art of paper cutting. The Polish people first started cutting their beautiful paper designs around the middle of the nineteenth century. They used the paper cuttings to make decorations for their homes.

Each year the peasants would take down the old paper cutouts, whitewash the walls of their homes, and put up their newly-made designs. The dusty ones might be put in the barn for the cows to enjoy.

Different regions of Poland have their own special paper-cutting designs. The Kurpie (koor-pye) region in northeast Poland is known for its symmetrical designs, cut from pieces of paper that have been folded in half.

Literature References

The Christmas Spider by Lovetta Holz; Philomel Books, 1980.
Feathers by Ruth Gordan; Macmillan, 1993.
Flowers on the Wall by Miriam Nerlove; M. K. McElderry Books, 1996.
Jacob's Rescue: A Holocaust Story by Malka Drucker and Michael Halperen; Bantam Books, 1993.
The Nine Crying Dolls: A Story from Poland by Anne Pellowski; Philomel Books, 1980.
Strudel, Strudel, Strudel by Steve Sanfield; Orchard Books, 1995.

Make Wycinanki Designs

- patterns on page 69
- colored copy paper
- 8" (20 cm) square of colored copy paper
- 6" (15 cm) square of white paper

- pencil
- scissors
- watered-down white glue
- small bowl or aluminum dish
- small paint brush

▶ **Steps to Follow**

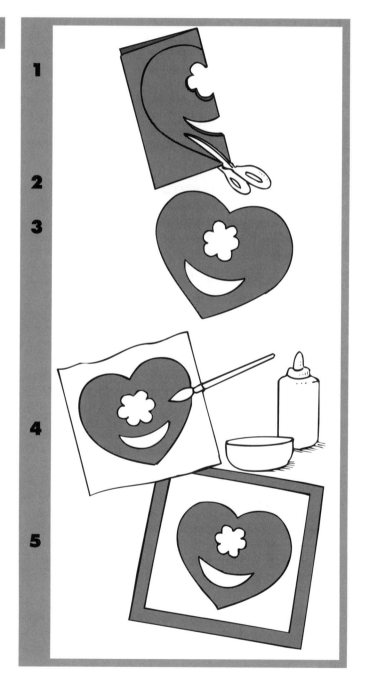

1. Reproduce the patterns on page 69 on colored copy paper. (One pattern is more complex and requires well-developed cutting skills.)

2. Cut around the box outline and fold the pattern square in half.

3. Carefully cut out and open the design.

4. Lay the design upside down on a piece of scrap paper. Paint on the watered-down white glue. Carefully lift the design and lay it on the white square. (Work in pairs for best results with this step.)

5. Glue the white square to the large colored square.

cut

cut

cut

fold

cut

fold

Folk Art Projects•Around the World EMC 721

Clay Rooster
Portugal

Portuguese peasants have been making these decorative sculptures since the Middle Ages. They first worked with stone and then later with clay. The sculptures are brilliantly colored with oil paints or lacquer. The rooster is one of the most popular subjects today because it is considered the harbinger of good luck.

Long ago in a region called Barcelos, an accused murderer was saved from the gallows by a rooster. The prisoner had made a last plea to a judge who was having dinner. If he were innocent, he said, the baked rooster on the judge's plate would get up and crow. And the rooster did just that!

The Portuguese people believe that black roosters are for "everyday" good luck. White roosters are given as wedding presents.

Literature Connections

The Girl, the Fish, and the Crown by Marilee Heyer; Viking, 1995.
Portugal by Esther Cross; Children's Press, 1986.
Portugal - in Pictures; Lerner Publications Co., 1991.

Make a Portuguese Rooster

▶ Materials

- 4" Styrofoam ball
- 1/2 of 4" Styrofoam ball
- 3" Styrofoam egg
- patterns on page 72
- poster board scraps
- cardboard tubes

- instant papier-mâché
- straight pins
- gesso
- acrylic paints
- masking tape

▶ Steps to Follow

Framework for rooster:

1. Roll a 4" (10 cm) tall cone from the poster board scraps.
2. Push the wide end of the cone into the rounded portion of the Styrofoam half-ball. This forms the base and the legs of the rooster.
3. Push the whole ball onto the narrow end of the cone for the body.
4. Slit the cardboard tube and rewind tightly so that it creates a paper tube with a 1" (2.5 cm) diameter. Cut off a 4" (10 cm) section.
5. Push the cut-off section of paper tube into the body to become the rooster's neck.
6. Push the Styrofoam egg onto the neck.
7. Cut two tails from the poster board using the pattern on page 72.
8. Tape the two tail pieces together except for the flaps.
9. Pin the flaps of the tail to the sides of the rooster body.
10. Cut two combs from the poster board. Tape the two combs together and push into the top of the rooster's head.
11. Cut out four poster board wattles. Tape in pairs to make two wattles. Push the waddles into the lower portion of the head on either side.
12. Add a beak made from a small cone of poster board. Push into head.

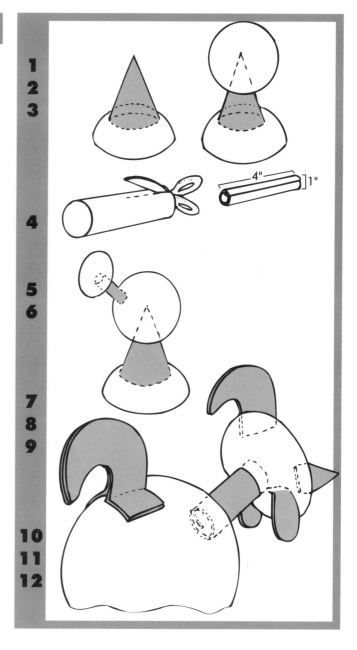

Finishing the rooster:

1. Cover the framework with a coat of instant papier mâché. Use a spoon to smooth the coat.

2. Dry completely. (Do not dry the rooster in the oven. The Styrofoam will expand and the sculpture will be destroyed.)

3. Apply two coats of gesso. Allow drying time between coats.

4. Paint the rooster with acrylic paints.

5. Spray with finishing coat.

1

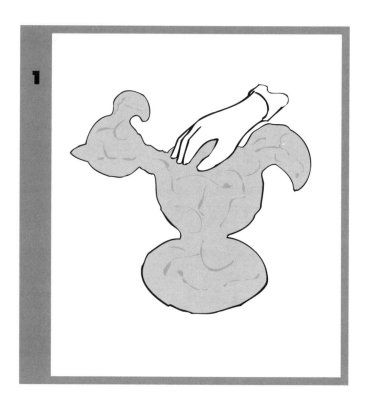

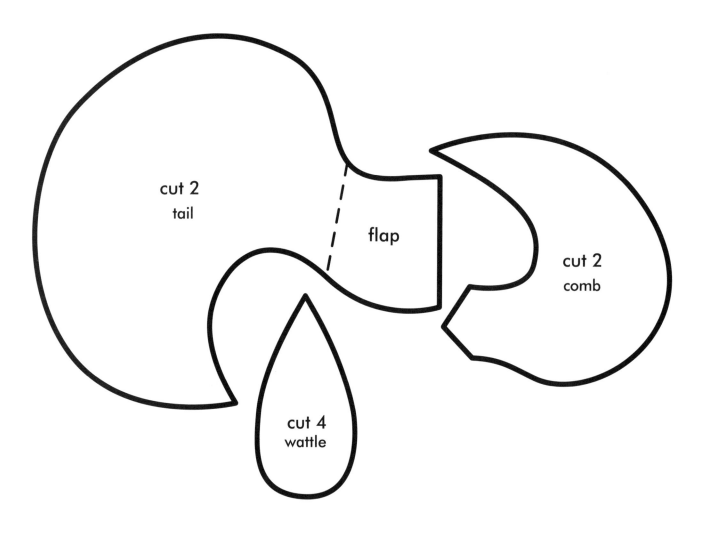

cut 2
tail

flap

cut 2
comb

cut 4
wattle

Ritz-Technick
Romania

The people of Romania have practiced the wood-decorating style called Ritz-Technik for thousands of years. This craft involves the scoring or incising of designs on a wood surface. The trademark of Romanian work is the geometric quality of their designs. Symmetrical patterns are composed of circles, semicircles, spirals, and crosses.

Literature Connections

The Enchanted Pig: A Rumanian Fairy Tale illustrated by Jacques Tardi; Creative Education, 1994.
The Gift of the Traveler by Wendy Matthews; BridgeWater Books, 1995.
Romania by Mark Sanborne; Facts on File, 1996.
Rumania by Sean Sheehan; Cavendish, 1994.
Uncertain Roads: Searching for Gypsies by Yale Storm; Four Winds Press, 1993.

Make a Ritz-Technick Design

▶ **Steps to Follow**

1. On a piece of scratch paper the same size as the balsa wood, develop the design that you will use. Use the samples on page 75 for ideas. Remember that the design should be geometric in nature. Romanian artisans use circles, semicircles, spirals, and crosses in symmetrical patterns. Think about symmetry as you are developing your design. Make sure that your design is the same on both sides.

2. Using a straightedge and circle tracers, draw your design on the balsa rectangle with the dull pencil. Press hard so that the design is "carved" into the wood.

3. When the design is completed, brush the wood with a watercolor wash so that the color goes into the carvings. Wipe the paint off with a damp sponge, so that the color retained in the carved areas is darker than the surface color.

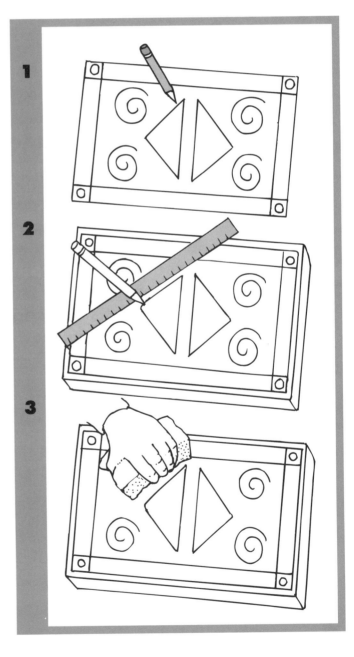

Finger Knotting
Switzerland

Swiss children learn to finger-knot when they are very young. They create long strands that can be shaped into little baskets, worn as bracelets, or used as key chains.

Literature Connections

Baby Crow by John A. Rowe; North-South Books, 1994.
The Beginning of the Armadillo by Rudyard Kipling; North-South Books, 1995.
The Christmas Angel by Pirkko Vainio; North-South Books, 1995.
Switzerland by Martin Hintz; Children's Press, 1986.
William Tell by Leonard Everett Fisher; Farrar, Straus & Giroux, 1996.

Make a Knotted Cord

▶ **Materials**

- cotton string or thin cording - an 8 ' (2.5 m) string will make an 18" (46 cm) cord

▶ **Steps to Follow**

1. Make a slip knot near one end of the cotton string.

2. Hold the loop in your left hand. With your right hand, push a new loop through the first loop. Pull the new loop with your right hand until the previous loop forms a knot. Adjust the size of the new loop by pulling on the free end of the cord with the right hand. Then repeat making new loops and knots until the cord is as long as you want.

3. Put the free end through the last loop. Pull tight.

▶ **Hints**

Use the cord as a bracelet for wrist or ankle, a decorative cord for a key, or a zipper pull.

Even tension on the two ends of the cord will make the knots even. You may want to tape the end of the cord down to keep it from twisting if you are working on a long cord.

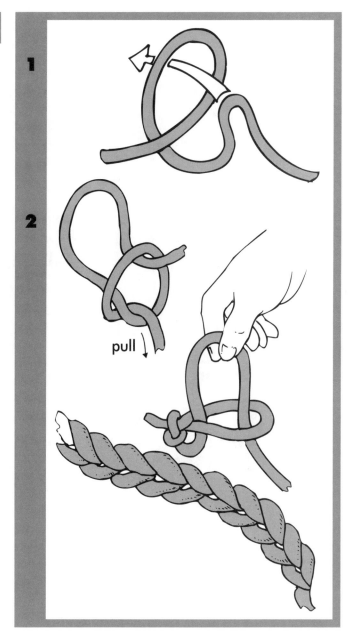

Pysanky
Ukraine

Legend has it that as long as pysanky are decorated, goodness will prevail over evil throughout the world. Pysanky is a special form of batik used for egg writing. Hot beeswax is applied onto a clean white egg, creating a specific pattern.

The egg is dipped into yellow dye. Then more wax writing is added. The wax writing alternates with a series of dippings into darker dyes. After the final dip, the egg is placed in a warm oven to melt the wax so that it can be easily wiped off to reveal the intricate design. A coat of clear acrylic spray seals the colors. This pysanky lesson substitutes crayons for wax and watercolors for the dyes.

Literature Connections

Baba Yaga and Vasilisa the Brave by Marianna Mayer; Morrow Junior Books, 1994.
The Firebird by Demi; Henry Holt, 1994.
First Snow, Magic Snow by John Cech; Four Winds Press, 1992.
Matreshka by Becky Hickox Ayres; Doubleday Books for Young Readers, 1992.
The Tsar's Promise retold by Robert D. San Souci; Philomel Books, 1992.

Make a Pysanky Egg

▶ **Materials**

- an egg shell (see page 80 for how to blow out an egg)
- yellow or white crayons
- water color paints - yellow, orange, red, black
- acrylic spray gloss

▶ **Steps to Follow**

1. Draw on the egg shell with a light colored crayon. Divide the shell into eight sections.

2. Paint or dip the egg into the yellow paint. Let the egg dry completely.

3. Add to the design with the crayon. Try filling in several of the areas that you have created.

4. Paint or dip the egg into the orange paint. Let the egg dry completely.

5. Add more to the design with the crayon.

6. Paint or dip the egg into the red paint. Let the egg dry completely.

7. Add to the design for the final time.

8. Paint or dip the egg into the black paint. Let the egg dry completely.

9. Heat the egg in the oven (200 degrees).

10. Gently rub to remove the wax.

11. Spray the egg with glossy acrylic spray.

How to blow out an egg:

1. Pierce each end of the egg with a needle.

2. Hold the egg over a bowl, poke the needle into the hole at the top to assure that the protective membrane has been broken. Then turn the egg over and gently blow out into the other end.

3. The yolk and the white should blow out into the bowl. If nothing happens, make the exit hole a little larger.

4. Wash the shell and let it dry.

▶ Hint

Prepare an egg stand before dying the eggs. Cut a circle from the bottom of an egg carton cup. Turn the cup upside down and balance the egg in the hole.